BASEBALL LEGENDS

Hank Aaron
Grover Cleveland Alexander
Ernie Banks
Johnny Bench
Yogi Berra
Roy Campanella
Roberto Clemente
Ty Cobb
Dizzy Dean
Joe DiMaggio
Bob Feller
Jimmie Foxx
Lou Gehrig
Bob Gibson
Rogers Hornsby
Walter Johnson
Sandy Koufax
Mickey Mantle
Christy Mathewson
Willie Mays
Stan Musial
Satchel Paige
Brooks Robinson
Frank Robinson
Jackie Robinson
Babe Ruth
Duke Snider
Warren Spahn
Willie Stargell
Honus Wagner
Ted Williams
Carl Yastrzemski
Cy Young

CHELSEA HOUSE PUBLISHERS

BASEBALL LEGENDS

CY YOUNG

Norman L. Macht

Introduction by
Jim Murray

Senior Consultant
Earl Weaver

CHELSEA HOUSE PUBLISHERS
New York • Philadelphia

Published by arrangement with
Chelsea House Publishers.
Newfield Publications is a federally
registered trademark of Newfield
Publications, Inc.

Produced by James Charlton Associates
New York, New York.

Designed by Hudson Studio
Ossining, New York.

Typesetting by LinoGraphics
New York, New York.

Picture research by Carolann Hawkins
Cover illustration by Dan O'Leary

CONTENTS

WHAT MAKES A STAR

Jim Murray

No one has ever been able to explain to me the mysterious alchemy that makes one man a .350 hitter and another player, more or less identical in physical makeup, hard put to hit .200. You look at an Al Kaline, who played with the Detroit Tigers from 1953 to 1974. He was pale, stringy, almost poetic-looking. He always seemed to be struggling against a bad case of mononucleosis. But with a bat in his hands, he was King Kong. During his career, he hit 399 home runs, rapped out 3,007 hits, and compiled a .297 batting average.

Form isn't the reason. The first time anybody saw Roberto Clemente step into the batter's box for the Pittsburgh Pirates, the best guess was that Clemente would be back in Double A ball in a week. He had one foot in the bucket and held his bat at an awkward angle—he looked as though he couldn't hit an outside pitch. A lot of other ballplayers may have had a better-looking stance. Yet they never led the National League in hitting in four different years, the way Clemente did.

Not every ballplayer is born with the ability to hit a curveball. Nor is exceptional hand-eye coordination the key to heavy hitting. Big-league locker rooms are filled with players who have all the attributes, save one: discipline. Every baseball man can tell you a story about a pitcher who throws a ball faster than anyone has ever seen but who has no control on or *off* the field.

The Hall of Fame is full of people who transformed themselves into great ballplayers by working at the sport, by studying the game, and making sacrifices. They're overachievers—and winners. If you want to find them, just watch the World Series. Or simply read about New York Yankee great Lou Gehrig; Ted Williams, "the Splendid Splinter" of the Boston Red Sox; or the Dodgers' strikeout king Sandy Koufax.

A pitcher *should* be able to win a lot of ballgames with a 98-miles-per-hour fastball. But what about the pitcher who wins 20 games a year with a fastball so slow that you can catch it with your teeth? Bob Feller of the Cleveland Indians got into the Hall of Fame with a blazing fastball that glowed in the dark. National League star Grover Cleveland Alexander got there with a pitch that took considerably longer to reach the plate; but when it did arrive, the pitch was exactly where Alexander wanted it to be—and the last place the batter expected it to be.

There are probably more players with exceptional ability who didn't make it to the major leagues than there are who did. A number of great hitters, bored with fielding practice, had to be dropped from their team because their home-run production didn't make up for their lapses in the field. And then there are players like Brooks Robinson of the Baltimore Orioles, who made himself into a human vacuum cleaner at third base because he knew that working hard to become an expert fielder would win him a job in the big leagues.

A star is not something that flashes through the sky. That's a comet. Or a meteor. A star is something you can steer ships by. It stays in place and gives off a steady glow; it is fixed, permanent. A star works at being a star.

And that's how you tell a star in baseball. He shows up night after night and takes pride in how brightly he shines. He's Willie Mays running so hard his hat keeps falling off; Ty Cobb sliding to stretch a single into a double; Lou Gehrig, after being fooled in his first two at-bats, belting the next pitch off the light tower because he's taken the time to study the pitcher. Stars never take themselves for granted. That's why they're stars.

THE FIRST WORLD SERIES

When Cy Young, a 36-year-old farmer from Ohio and a pitcher for the Boston Pilgrims (now called the Red Sox), threw the first ball in the 1903 World Series, he had no idea that he was launching an annual sports event that would someday be watched by a billion people around the world. It was not even called the World Series back then. Nor did it become an annual contest until two years later.

The National League had been the only major league for 25 years, until 1901, when another group decided to start a rival circuit. This new league, called the American League, raided the National League's teams and signed many of its star players. Not surprisingly, there was bitter fighting between the two leagues and a steady stream of lawsuits for two years. The two leagues finally signed a peace treaty in 1903, and the raids stopped. But the Americans and Nationals

For the opener of the first World Series ever, fans crowded the infield to watch fielding practice at Boston's Huntington Avenue Grounds. The field was home to the Pilgrims until Fenway Park was opened in 1912.

still would have nothing to do with each other.

Cy Young had been one of the National League players who had jumped to the American League. A perennial 20-game winner, he had spent 10 years in the N. L., the last two with the St. Louis Cardinals. But he had never liked the hot, humid climate of St. Louis. And he was not at all happy with his salary of $2,400 a year. So when the Boston Americans offered him $3,500 a year, he accepted. For the next three years Cy Young was the top pitcher in the new league, winning a total of 93 games against 30 losses. During that time, he finished all but six of the games he started.

Boston won the 1903 pennant easily, while the powerful Pittsburgh Pirates walked off with their third straight National League title. The owners of the two winners agreed to play a nine-game series; the first team to win five games would be recognized as America's baseball champion.

The opening game in Boston was a gala occasion. On a warm, sunny day, the downtown streets were decorated with flags and bunting. Boston fans gathered in the lobby of the Vendome Hotel and taunted the visiting players, who answered back by calling the Boston ace, Cy Young, an old man.

By early afternoon, more than 16,000 people had traveled to the ballpark and packed themselves into the little wooden grandstand that was intended for half that number. Many fans lined up along the foul lines and stood jammed together behind ropes in the outfield. Any batter who hit the ball into the crowd would automatically be given a three-base hit. To help make this happen, the hometown fans edged closer to the

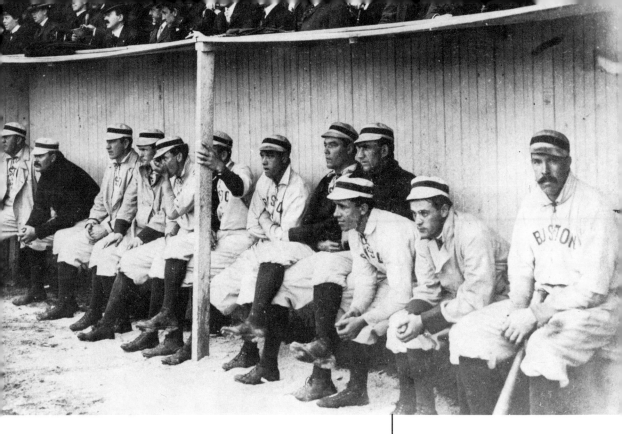

field whenever a Pirate outfielder raced toward them for a fly ball.

There was no public-address system in those days, and no radio or television. Before the game, a man held a megaphone to his mouth and announced each team's starting pitcher and catcher to the crowd: "For Pittsburgh, Phillippe and Phelps. For Boston, Young and Criger."

Postseason play was not a novelty to Cy Young. Back in 1894, when he was pitching for the Cleveland Spiders, the National League had begun an annual series between the first and second place teams for a trophy called the Temple Cup. The Spiders finished second in 1895 and 1896. After those two series, Young's record stood at 3–1.

The 1903 series offered a different kind of challenge. The American League felt it had some-

Cy Young (far left) and first baseman Candy LaChance (far right) flank the Boston bench during the opening game of the 1903 World Series. In the final game, a fight occured after a throw by LaChance hit a Pittsburgh player in the back.

thing to prove. Its teams were still being scoffed at by the National League teams, which resented losing so many of their best players to the American League.

The crowd cheered lustily when Cy Young went out to the mound to start the game, but they soon quieted down. His nervous teammates made four errors in the first inning, and the visitors scored four runs. Young, who had thrown the first pitch in World Series history, also gave up the first World Series home run (to an outfielder named Jimmy Sebring). The Pirates won the opener, 7–3. Bill Dinneen then pitched a 3–0 shutout for Boston in game 2 to even the series.

The third game was played on a Saturday, and almost 19,000 fans crowded their way into the ballpark to see the action. After the Pirates took an early lead, Young was sent in to pitch. He hurled seven innings in relief, but Boston lost again, 4–2.

After three games in Boston, the teams traveled by train to Pittsburgh. The journey took more than 24 hours, and they had to change trains twice along the way. More than 200 of Boston's most loyal fans, known as the Royal Rooters, followed their heroes to Pittsburgh. After the Pirates won game 4 and took a 3–1 lead in the series, their fans presented the Royal Rooters with a big colorful umbrella. The Rooters paraded around the field with the umbrella after Cy Young pitched an 11–2 victory in game 5. The next day, Bill Dinneen hurled a 6 – 3 win to beat Pittsburgh's Sam Leever, a 25-game winner during the regular season.

Two days later, with the series tied at 3–3, Young was again ready to pitch. This time he was matched against Deacon Phillippe, the winning pitcher in all three Pirates victories. It was a cold afternoon, but the Pittsburgh park was filled.

Before the game, two men approached Young on the crowded field. One of them said, "Young, we have a proposition for you. If you ease up and lose the game, there will be $20,000 in it for you. Our people have a lot of money bet on Pittsburgh."

Gambling on baseball games was widespread at the time, and there were a few players who did not hesitate to agree to this kind of offer. Twenty thousand dollars was equal to five years' worth of salary.

Young replied, "If you fellows value your money, put your bet on me. I'm going to win that game." And he did, 7–3.

Back in Boston, Bill Dinneen pitched the Pilgrims to their fourth straight victory. The Pilgrims had won the first World Series. Boston fans, led by the Royal Rooters, lifted their ace pitchers, Young and Dinneen, on their shoulders and carried them around the field. Cy Young and the upstart American Leaguers had proved they deserved equal standing with the proud Nationals.

2

GROWING UP ON THE FARM

Denton True Young was born on March 29, 1867, on a farm near Gilmore, Ohio. He was named Denton for an uncle who had gone out west during the gold rush of the 1840s. The name True was in honor of a Union army officer his father had served with in the Civil War.

Dent Young grew up as millions of farmboys did in the years following the war. Although he went off each spring for 22 years to play baseball, Young remained a farmer all his life and returned to the Ohio hills every winter. But that was not unusual in his time. Most Americans lived on farms or in small towns surrounded by farmland.

Dent did all the chores, beginning at five o'clock in the morning, milking the cows and feeding the livestock. After school, he chopped wood and worked in the fields until evening, when it was time to milk and feed the animals again. Dent's four brothers and one sister had similar responsibilities.

In the winter, when the water troughs froze over, Dent had to get up even earlier to chop the

Following the 1892 season, during which Cy Young won 36 games, new rules were introduced. The 4 by 5½ foot pitching box was replaced by a pitching rubber 60 feet 6 inches from home plate. The pitching rubber was five feet in back of the front line of the pitching box, but the added distance did not affect Young at all; he won 34 games in 1893.

15

ice so the animals could drink. He walked for miles in the snow, hunting deer and foxes. In the fall, he cut and husked the corn.

In his free time, Dent loved to throw things. He hung milk pails on the barn door and threw green apples, walnuts, rocks, whatever was at hand, until the pails were so banged up they could not be used for milking.

"All us Youngs could throw," he remembered. "When I was a kid I could kill squirrels with a stone. And my granddad once killed a turkey buzzard with a rock."

On spring afternoons, there was always a ballgame in the schoolyard. The boys did not have any real equipment. Their ball was made by wrapping old stockings around a black walnut. Their bat was a stick cut from a round hickory limb. They never owned gloves.

While in Nebraska, Young (left) pitched for a semi-pro team in St. Mary's.

Dent grew tall and broad-shouldered, topping 6 feet, 2 inches and 200 pounds. By the time he was 18, the farm began to look kind of small to him. He wanted to see what the West was like.

After a three-day ride on a train, Dent got off at Red Cloud, Nebraska, in the middle of the flat plains. He worked on a farm and pitched for the local Red Cloud team for $50 a month. It was 1885, and "road trips" for baseball teams in Nebraska were mostly made on muleback. Dent rode many a mule over dusty trails to get to a game.

He remained out west for three years, then got homesick for the hills of Ohio. He was happy to be back working on his father's farm for $10 a month and his keep. But baseball was also in his blood. When the farm chores were done and there was still enough daylight, he knew where to find a game. Every town had a team and lots of avid fans. For most people, baseball was the only form of daytime entertainment. Denton Young was in great demand as a pitcher, sometimes earning a dollar a game.

When he was not pitching, Young played in the infield and outfield. But he really did not shine there. At least one major-league scout looked him over when he was playing third base for the Tuscarawas County nine and concluded the big youngster could handle a plow better than a hot grounder. Of course, fielding in the late 19th century was a lot different from today. Most players did not wear gloves in the field; they were new pieces of equipment that were very expensive.

About this time, Young heard that the Tri-State League's professional team in Canton, Ohio, was holding open tryouts. He figured he would see what the pros thought of his pitching.

"It was a two-hour drive from our farm to Canton," he recalled, "so I arose early and was at the old boarded-in ballpark by 9:30. The manager said, 'I've heard about you, young fellow. Now let us see what you can do.'"

Dressed in his blue overalls, Young walked to the mound and fired off a string of fastballs so hard they went right past the catcher and splintered the boards in the fence behind home plate. The scouts and newspapermen watched and shook their heads.

"Just look at that fence," somebody said. "It looks like a cyclone hit it."

The label "Cyclone" Young was soon shortened, and nobody called Dent Young anything but Cy for the rest of his life.

The next day, Canton's manager rode 50 miles to the Youngs' farm to sign Cy to a contract. The manager was willing to pay Cy $40 a month. Cy's father thought it over and said no. There was no future in baseball, he said; his son's place was on the farm. It took Cy Young a few weeks to change his father's mind. He also persuaded the Canton club to raise its offer.

Young got off to a fast start at Wheeling, West Virginia, on the morning of April 30, 1890. He gave up just three hits in Canton's 4–2 victory. Young, however, had not yet gained the near-perfect control he would later become famous for, and in the next three months he lost as many games as he won. Then, on July 25, he pitched a no-hitter against McKeesport, striking out 18 and walking none.

Word of the hard-throwing farmer quickly spread. In the 1890s, one of the biggest men in baseball was Adrian "Cap" Anson. A star first

Cy Young at age 21.

baseman for the Chicago Colts for 22 years, he was also their manager. When Anson heard the raves about Young, he went to Canton to look him over. Unfortunately, Cy Young was wilder than usual that day. Anson admired his ability to throw hard, but he concluded that Young was just another farmer who would not make the grade in the big leagues. So even though Canton was willing to sell Young's contract for just $500, Anson turned him down.

The Canton Club was so low on cash that when the Cleveland club offered $250 for Young, they took it. Cleveland had joined the National League in 1889, and when Cy Young joined them in the middle of the 1890 season, the team was known as the Spiders.

There was nothing spidery about Young, though. Now 23, he was as broad as the side of a barn. He seemed to be outgrowing his clothes even as he sat on the train to Cleveland. When he arrived, his wrists hung down inches below his coat sleeves and his ankles stuck out beneath his trousers. The first thing Spider manager Gus Schmelz did was take him shopping for a new suit.

Young worked out at the ballpark until the Spiders returned from a road trip. Schmelz, who sported a big, bushy beard, told Cy he would make his first start against Cap Anson's mighty Chicago Colts on August 6. Young was eager to show the great Anson that he was more than just another farmboy.

The Spiders had to scrounge around to find a uniform that might come close to fitting the big pitcher. When Young appeared on the field he inspired more laughter than confidence. One newpaper reported: "As the players came from the clubhouse for practice, an uncouth figure that brought a giggle from the stands shambled along behind them. It was Denton T. Young, the new 'phenom.' Darius Green, the Pied Piper, and other noted characters of fact and fiction had nothing on Young for weirdness of appearance. The baseball knickerbockers he wore had been made for a man many inches shorter. His jersey shirt stretched across his massive body like a drumhead, and his arms dangled through its sleeves almost to the shoulder. He dragged himself across the field bashfully, every angle of his great frame exaggerated and emphasized."

The Chicago players, led by Anson, jeered and taunted Young. But when Young's fastball cracked into the catcher's thin glove, and the Chicago batters shook their heads and trailed their bats in the dust after striking out, the laughter and jeers soon stopped. Young allowed just three hits as the Spiders triumphed, 8–1. Young derived special satisfaction from the fact that he struck out Cap Anson twice.

That night in the hotel, Anson offered the Cleveland manager $2,000 for Young's contract. But he was too late. Schmelz was pretty sure that his young rookie was worth a whole lot more than that.

3

LIFE IN THE BIG LEAGUES

Life in the big leagues was no picnic in the 1890s. The playing fields were often full of stones, and there were no showers or lockers at the parks. Players would don their uniform at the hotel, climb aboard a horse-drawn streetcar or walk to the park, then return to their rooms after the game still wearing their dirty, sweaty uniforms.

For the most part, players stayed in noisy rooming houses, often sharing a bed with a teammate. Ballplayers were known for their rowdy ways, and the better hotels would not let them in the door.

But Cy Young was a quiet young man. He did not seem to fit with the Spiders, who were the roughest, brawlingest bunch in the league. The Spiders fought with rival players and spectators. Once, the entire team was arrested for starting a riot after a scrap with an umpire.

Built in 1883, Boston's magnificent Grand Pavilion was one of the most beautiful parks of its day. During a Boston–Baltimore game in May 1894, a tossed cigarette caused a fire that burned down the double-decked grandstand.

*Many years after Young
stopped pitching, the poet
Ogden Nash wrote:*
   Y is for Young
   The Magnificent Cy
   People batted against him,
   But I never knew why.

For many years only one umpire officiated in a game. Stationed behind the pitcher, there was no way he could keep an eye on everything. One day, Young was pitching against the Baltimore Orioles, and John McGraw was on first base. When the next batter hit a single, McGraw went from first to third by cutting straight across the field behind the umpire. The ump did not see it, but the Spiders' left fielder did. While the rest of the team was arguing with the ump, he ran in, took the ball from Young, knocked McGraw off third base, sat on his stomach, and tagged him out. The umpire then called McGraw out, and another argument began.

Baseball had always attracted gamblers, and they did not like to lose. Young had his first brush with them while pitching in Louisville. The home team was ahead by just one run when the Spiders loaded the bases with none out.

Before the next man came to bat, three gamblers, sitting just behind the catcher in the tiny ballpark, jumped to their feet. "If Louisville loses this game, there won't be enough left of you to worry about," one of them called to the umpire. Another waved a large pistol to underline the threat. Although the sun was still high in the sky, the umpire immediately called the game on account of darkness. As he ran off the field, the Spiders assaulted him with such high-spirited language that five of them were arrested and fined by a judge before they could leave town. That was one game Cy Young did not win.

Umpires were not the only ones who had problems. Consider the poor batters. Hitters seldom saw a clean white ball to hit except on the first pitch of the game. Unlike many other pitchers, Young did not throw a spitball; but he did chew a plug of tobacco, and the brown juice sometimes found its way onto the ball, which became softer and darker with each inning. Home runs were rare, and a foul ball hit into the stands had to be thrown back so the game could continue.

After his successful debut against Cap Anson's Colts, Young struggled along, losing as often as he won. His record was 7–7 going into the last day of the 1890 season. He won the first game of a doubleheader against the Phils, 5–1, then volunteered to pitch the second game as well. A 7–3 victory in that game gave him a 9–7 mark for his rookie year.

...h TO R

PS PITCHER, JOE McGINNITY PITCHER, PAT CHRISHAM CATCHER, GEO LaCHANCE 1ST B. HARRY HOWELL PITCHER, IN

W L TO R. DUCKY HOLMES L.F. BROADWAY ALEX SMITH CATCHER, WALTER STEVE BRODIE C.F. JOHN J McG

RY ROBINSON captain & CATCHER, CHARLIE CHICK HARRIS UTILITY INFIELD STEVE McKENNA PITC

ROW L TO R. DAVE FULTZ OUTFIELD, GENE DE MONTREVILLE 2ND B. BILLY KEISTER S.S. (JIMM

4

THE BEST PITCHER IN BASEBALL

Over 9,000 spectators were on hand to watch Cy Young pitch his first big-league Opening Day game in Cleveland. The home fans went away happy as the Spiders beat the Reds, 12–3, for the first of Young's 27 wins in 1891.

The next year, he was almost unbeatable, posting 36 victories against 11 losses. The National League played a split season; Boston won the first half, and the Spiders were the second-half champions. In the playoff for the pennant, however, the Boston Beaneaters, later called the Braves, won all five games.

Young spent little time brooding over the loss. He had other things on his mind. On November 8, 1892, he married Robba Miller, who grew up on a neighboring farm across the town line in Peoli. Young then bought her father's farm, and the newlyweds moved into the original farm-

The Baltimore Orioles of 1899, the last season Baltimore fielded a major-league team until 1954. The old Orioles, led by John McGraw (second row, center), combined speed, aggressiveness, and hostility to win three pennants in the 1890s. In 1902, the combative McGraw began managing the New York Giants, a job he held for 30 years.

house. It had been built more than a hundred years earlier, from timber sawed out by horse power and worked down by hand. Robba Young often traveled with her husband when the team was on the road. She knew her baseball and was an avid fan.

For the next six years, Cy Young gave all his fans something to cheer about. He twice won more than 30 games. In those days, a team carried only four or five pitchers, less than half the number that teams now carry, and each was expected to pitch often and to finish every game he started. Young rarely failed to complete a game. During this time, he perfected the control that made him one of the sharpest pitchers around. For 22 years he would average fewer than two walks per game.

In addition to his fastball, Young threw two kinds of curves that broke in different ways and baffled the batters. His favorite pitch was a whistler under the chin that discouraged hitters from relaxing at the plate.

In 1892, Young threw nine shutouts, a remarkable number when you consider that most teams made about three or four errors per game. One year, he pitched 15 games on a 23-game road trip and won 11 of them.

In 1896, the Spiders got a new catcher, Lou Criger, who would play a big part in Young's future success. "A catcher can make or break his pitcher," Young once said. "The pitcher and catcher must work together as one."

The 1897 season was disappointing for Young. His record slipped from the previous year's 29–16 to 21–18. But his spirits were boosted on September 18, when he pitched a 6 – 0 no-hitter against the Reds. It was the league's first no-hitter in four years.

Young's record improved to 25–14 in 1898, but the Spiders finished fifth for the second straight year. Attendance dropped, and the club lost money. It did not help that it was against the law to play baseball on Sundays in Cleveland. Because most people had to work six days a week, Sunday was the only day they could get out to the ballpark. Sunday games were legal in St. Louis, however, so the Cleveland owners bought the St. Louis team and moved most of their players, including Young, to that city for the next season. They continued to own the Spiders, too. (There was no rule against owning two teams in the same league.) But they left such poor players in Cleveland that the 1899 Spiders managed only 20 victories while losing 134

Cy Young with Lou Criger. Young said of his catcher, "As a backstop, as a thrower, for quick intelligent action, he ranks with the best who have ever handled a ball." Watching the two is a leader of the Royal Rooters, "Nuf Ced" McGreevey, who got his nickname by ending baseball arguments with "enough said."

Former boxer John L. Sullivan (left), "The Boston Strongboy," sits in the Pilgrims' dugout with Boston player-manager Jimmy Collins before the start of the 1903 Series. Sullivan was the heavyweight champion for 10 years until he was knocked out by James J. Corbett after 21 rounds in 1892.

games, the worst team record in major-league history.

As the ace of the pitching staff, Cy Young was picked to pitch the first game in St. Louis. The day was cold and windy, but nearly 18,000 people filled the grandstand and ringed the outfield. Young's opponents were the forlorn Spiders. Sporting new uniforms with bright red trim and stockings, the newly named St. Louis Cardinals won easily, 10–1. Their name, their colors, and their home park had changed, but inside they were still the same old rough and tough players.

"It surely is great trying to score a run on that infield," moaned a rival player. "You get on first and [Patsy] Tebeau gives you the shoulder. You pass second and [Clarence "Cupid"] Childs gives you the hip. Shortstop Big Ed McLean tries to trip you if he thinks the umpire isn't looking and they've even got that mild Rhoddy Wallace giving you his spikes at third. And at the plate, [catcher Jack] O'Connor will do anything short of murder to keep you from scoring."

Despite their good start, the Cardinals gradually slipped to fifth place. And even though Young wound up with a winning 26–15 record, he was not happy in St. Louis. He did not like the intense heat and muggy atmosphere of the city on the banks of the Mississippi River.

In 1900, the Cards finished sixth, and Cy Young won 20 against 18 losses, his worst performance in 10 years. That winter, Young received a letter from the American League's Boston team, offering him $3,500 to play for them. That was more money than he had ever earned.

Young felt a strong loyalty to the St. Louis club and his teammates, but he was now 34 and did not know how long he could continue to earn a living playing ball. Besides, he much preferred the cooler weather of New England. So when he heard that his favorite catcher, Lou Criger, was going to Boston, the scales definitely tipped in Boston's favor. Young signed the contract. He could not know that, while he was worrying about how much longer he would be able to pitch, his greatest years were still ahead of him.

5

THE PERFECT GAME

A few weeks after Theodore Roosevelt was inaugurated as president in 1901, the American League made its debut. Cy Young's new team, called the Puritans for a while, then the Somersets and the Pilgrims, had signed enough top stars to make it a hardhitting, scrappy contender. More than 11,000 people stormed the new ballpark for the opening game, and Young rewarded them with a 12–4 win. That same afternoon, only 2,000 showed up to watch the National League's Beaneaters play a few blocks away.

Cy won 33 and lost 10 as Boston stayed in the pennant race until the last week, then settled for second place. The next year, his record dipped slightly, to 32–11, and the team finished third. But the team put it all together in 1903. This time, they ran away from the pack, leaving Philadelphia 14 ½ games behind. Uncle Cy, as the younger players now called him, was 36 years old, but he won 28 while losing only 9, pitched more innings than anybody else, and

The Royal Rooters band, a raucous bunch that serenaded friend and foe alike. Some of the Pirates credited them with winning the 1903 World Series for Boston.

threw 7 shutouts. A good hitter, he also batted .321.

With their superior play, the Pilgrims had won over most of Boston's fans and cut so sharply into the N.L. Beaneaters' attendance that the Nationals gave up the battle. They signed an agreement that ended the player raids and recognized the American as an equal major league. The success of the 1903 championship series, arranged between the owners of the Boston Americans and the Pittsburgh Nationals, spotlighted the benefits of cooperation. Young's success in those games was a high point in his career.

After 14 years of big-league ball, it seemed that Cy Young had done just about everything there was to accomplish. But then, in 1904, he turned in the most spectacular achievements of his career.

Young's biggest rival for pitching honors in the early years of the American League was Rube Waddell of the Philadelphia Athletics. An eccentric left-hander, Waddell threw the sharpest curves and swiftest fastballs of them all. But off the field, he was anything but sharp. In fact, he was downright flakey. Waddell chased fire engines racing to fires, wrestled alligators, shot marbles with kids under the grandstand when he was supposed to be warming up, and went fishing whenever he felt like it. When he felt like pitching, however, Rube Waddell was just about unhittable. Anytime he and Cy Young squared off, crowds flocked to the park in anticipation of a brilliant duel between the two aces.

The 10,000 fans who packed the Boston park on May 5, 1904, were not disappointed. Two days earlier, Waddell had pitched a one-hitter against the Pilgrims. To top that, Young would have to be perfect. And he was. Not one Philadelphia batter reached first base that day: no hits, no walks, no errors. In the past 100 years, there have been only a dozen such games pitched. The score was 3–0, and it was all over in an hour and 23 minutes. Waddell, the last of the Athletics to face him, hit a long fly ball to center field for the final out. The fans poured onto the field, trying to get close enough to shake Young's hand.

That perfect game set Young up for one of baseball's most enduring records. On April 25, Young had lost to Waddell, 2–0, the only two runs coming in the first inning. The Athletics had been hitless in the 8th and 9th. Then, on April 30, Young had pitched seven innings in relief and given up no runs or hits. Six days after his perfect game, Uncle Cy shut out Detroit for 15 innings and won, 1–0. The Tigers did not get

The announced attendance for game 3 of the 1903 Series was 18,801, yet the Boston Globe *reported that more than 23,000 were at the game. This photo of fans climbing over the outfield fence helps explain the difference.*

Boston won the American League pennant in 1904 with a doubleheader split over the New York Highlanders on the last day of the season. But John McGraw refused to allow his National League Giants to face Boston in the World Series.

a hit until the 7th. And on May 17, Cleveland was scoreless against him until the 8th inning. When the scorekeepers added it all up, that came to 23 $^2/_3$ consecutive hitless innings for Young, and 45 without a run being scored off him. That record for consecutive shutout innings stood until Don Drysdale topped it with 58 in 1968.

Cy Young finished the 1904 season with 26 wins, 10 of them shutouts. That same season, he struck out 200 and walked only 29 in 43 games. But Young paced himself and did not try to strike out every batter, and he did not mind giving up hits. When a rookie pitcher asked him how he did it, Young said, "I do the best I can with the ball up to the time it leaves my hand, and after that it is up to the batter."

Boston won the pennant again in 1904, and the New York Giants topped the National League.

But the Giants refused to play in the World Series. Boston and New York fans alike were eager for the confrontation. They set up a mighty howl, demanding a playoff. But John McGraw and the Giant management would not budge. Their response to the Pilgrim challenge was: "We don't play minor leaguers." It would be another year before the World Series began its uninterrupted run.

At about this time, the players were frequenting a little drugstore near the ballpark owned by a man named Frederick Putnam. Cy Young suggested that Putnam open a hotel next to the store, so the players would have a convenient place to stay. Putnam took his advice, and the Youngs and other players made Putnam's hotel their home as long as they were in Boston. Putnam prospered, and many years later he would return the favor.

In the meantime, Young had saved enough money to buy a 160-acre farm and build a grand home in Peoli. He continued to work on the farm and to walk many miles that winter, as he looked forward to another successful season.

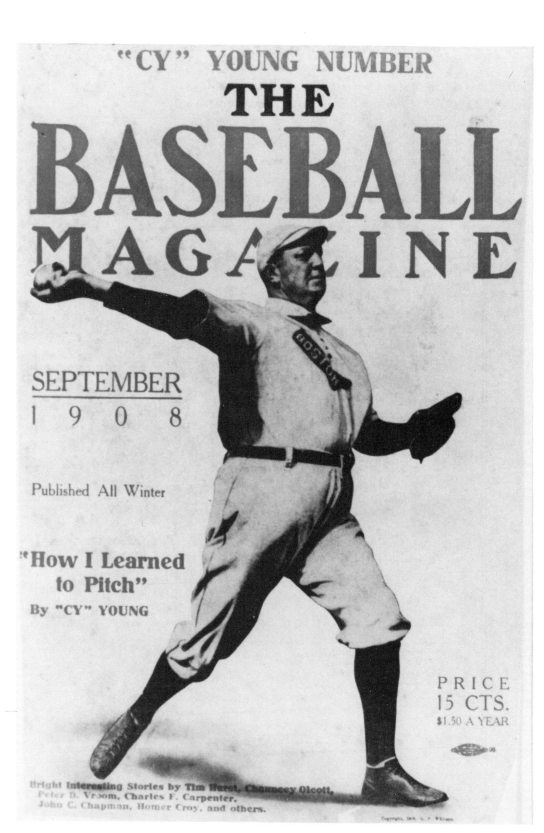

"CY" YOUNG NUMBER

THE BASEBALL MAGAZINE

SEPTEMBER
1 9 0 8

Published All Winter

"How I Learned
to Pitch"
By "CY" YOUNG

PRICE
15 CTS.
$1.50 A YEAR

Bright Interesting Stories by Tim Hurst, Chauncey Olcott,
Peter D. Vroom, Charles F. Carpenter,
John C. Chapman, Homer Croy, and others.

Copyright, 1908, G. F. Wilson

6

CY YOUNG HAS HIS DAY

The 1905 season was not a triumphant one. The team had a new owner, and there was friction between him and the manager, Jimmy Collins. The best players missed a lot of games due to injuries and illness. Cy Young pitched as well as ever, striking out 208 and walking only 30 in 320 innings. But he could not do it all alone. With little support from his teammates, his record fell below .500 for the first time: 18–19.

The Fourth of July, 1905, was a different story. The holiday custom at the time was to play a game in the morning and another in the afternoon. It was a hot day in Boston. The Athletics had won the morning game, and Young and Waddell were scheduled to pitch in the afternoon.

Young pitched his then-record third no-hitter (under modern rules) on June 30, 1908. "A pitcher's got to be good," Cy said, "and he's got to be lucky to get a no-hit game."

There was not one empty seat or standing room for another fan when Cy Young tossed the first pitch. Both hurlers were nicked for an early pair of runs, but then they began to hang up the goose eggs. The game quickly went into extra innings, each man seldom needing more than 10

Young's pitching rival, Rube Waddell, was not the most disciplined ballplayer, but, in the words of Branch Rickey, "when Waddell had control — and some sleep — he was unbeatable." His 1904 single-season-strikeout mark of 349 lasted 69 years until Nolan Ryan struck out 383 in 1973.

pitches to set down the side. In the 14th inning, Young was struck on the arm by a line drive. The arm began to swell and a dark bruise emerged, but he shook off the pain. Meanwhile, Waddell was having his own troubles. Whenever the Bostons threatened, their fans set off firecrackers and fired pistols in the air. But Rube Waddell took it in stride. Nothing rattled him.

The innings peeled away: 15, 16, 17, 18, 19. Young had not walked a single batter, while Waddell had struck out a dozen. Neither man wilted in the heat or tired from throwing more than 200 pitches. In the top of the 20th, Cy Young threw his only bad pitch of the day and hit a batter. Then he booted a ground ball. His fielders, who had bailed him out of a few tight spots with remarkable plays, flagged a little and made another error. A timely single produced two runs for the visitors. Waddell then shut down the home team and staggered off the field with a 4–2 victory.

Even Cy Young was weary after that one. Asked how he felt at the end of the long, hot game, he said, "Well, I thought it was all right until I hit the clubhouse. Then I all but keeled over. When I sat down and tried to get up it was as if there was a pain in every part of my body. Then, when I tried to take off my shoe, I hardly had strength to untie the laces."

The next day, his arm was sore where it had been bruised, but otherwise he felt fine. "For my part, I think it was the greatest game of ball I ever took part in," Young said later. "I, of course, would like to have won it, but it has been my practice to take things as they come, and I have no kick coming that we did not win."

Win or lose, that 20-inning pitchers' duel was a bright spot during a dismal season in which Boston finished fourth.

Dismal turned to dreary in 1906. Manager Jimmy Collins, who had led the team from the start, announced that he was quitting, was talked into staying on, then quit for good. Boston fell all the way into the cellar, losing 105 games against just 49 wins. Young won 13 and lost 21, his worst record ever.

Cy Young was 39, and as the long summer dragged to a close, he began to think about ending his career. But his arm was still sound, and he did not want to leave the game on a losing note. He believed he could still get the batters out, but the team would have to contribute more runs if he was going to win 20 again.

Young trained more diligently than ever that winter, determined to get off to a strong start in the spring. The new manager, 33-year-old Chick Stahl, was a popular outfielder who had jumped from the Beaneaters to the American League in 1901. The team was filled with optimism during spring training. Then they heard the shocking news: Chick Stahl had killed himself. The stunned, leaderless players sat staring at the ground. Nobody had an explanation or knew what to say.

The club owner asked Cy Young to take charge as manager. He was the most respected man on the team. But Young did not want the job. "Judging from the way I have been going this spring," he explained, "I believe I will have one of my best seasons this year, and I would not have anything worrying me. I also believe I do not have the ability to manage the team. I feel highly honored, but I could not do justice to both positions."

Young agreed to run the team until another man could be found. He was the manager for the first seven games, three of which were won by Boston. Two other managers came and went before one arrived to finish the year. Although the team wound up in seventh place, Cy Young did stage his comeback. He worked 343 innings with 22 wins and proved he was as strong at the age of 40 as he had been at 30.

There was one ray of hope at the end of the season for the Pilgrims, but it was a star still too dim and distant to shed much light. A 19-year-old outfielder named Tris Speaker joined the team. A future Hall of Famer, he was one of the many young players who benefitted from Cy Young's experience.

"He'd take me out on the practice field and hit fungos to me by the hour," Speaker said. "I got to watching and studying his swing, and by doing that I learned to start after the ball before he actually hit it."

Along with the technical tips, Uncle Cy passed along these simple rules to the future star: "Live a temperate life. Do not abuse yourself if you want to attain success. Do not try to bait the umpires. Play the game for all you are worth at all times. Render faithful service to your employers."

Old Cy Young still had some magic up his sleeve. He no longer had the speed of his youth, but he had knowledge and experience. On June 30, 1908, he took the mound against the New York Highlanders, who would soon become known as the Yankees. (By then, the Pilgrims were generally referred to by their new name, the Red Sox.)

Young walked the first New York batter he faced, who then was cut down trying to steal

Young with the trophy given to him on his "day" in 1908.

The costumed battery of Young (left) and Lou Criger before marching on the field for Cy Young Day celebrations on August 13, 1908.

second base. Young then set down the next 26 batters. Except for that first batter, it would have been another perfect game. As it was, another Cy Young no-hitter went into the books. Young not only kept the Highlanders off base, he contributed 3 hits to his team's 8–0 victory.

After this third no-hitter, Boston fans were delirious with appreciation and love for the old man. A local newspaper proposed a day honoring Cy Young, and the fans took it up immediately. A campaign was launched to raise money for a silver trophy. Young was so popular with players on other teams that they chipped in to buy him a trophy, too. And the umpires, who never heard a word of complaint from him, presented him with a suitcase. The value of his gifts far exceeded his annual salary of $4,500 a year.

Stars from other teams traveled to Boston to play in an all-star game, the first time that was ever done. When the gates opened at 11:30 on the morning of August 13, 1908, more than 20,000 people squeezed into the grandstand. The doors had to be closed with another 10,000 clamoring to get in. The sale of tickets brought in $7,500, and that too was given to Young.

Before the game, the players dressed in costumes and marched around the field. Cy Young led the parade, dressed in farmer's overalls and a set of bushy false whiskers. Others wore cowboy, soldier, and Uncle Sam getups.

After the gift-giving was finished, Young stood at home plate, shouting his thanks to the crowd. (And that winter he wrote a personal letter to each of the hundreds who had contributed to the cost of the fans' trophy.) Young pitched the first three innings for the Red Sox against the all-stars, which the stars won, 3–2, in 11 innings. It was the most festive day baseball had ever seen and the most memorable of Cy Young's long career. Winning the affection of the people meant a lot more to him than winning the game.

7

END OF THE LINE

C y Young had been Boston's best pitcher in 1908, with a 21–11 record. But the years were catching up with him. So he was not surprised one winter's evening when a reporter walked into the barn where he was milking the cows and broke the news to him: Young had been traded to Cleveland. His first reaction was, "I'm sorry to leave Boston, but I'm glad I'm going back to Cleveland where I made my start, where I have always been treated with the utmost kindness."

Young milked the cows in silence for a while, then added, "I don't expect I'll be leaving the farm many seasons more. When a farmer gets to be 42 he begins to long for home and begins to dread the long bumps and the long days in the hotels that are part of a ballplayer's life. I shan't be sorry when the time comes for me to settle down here."

The Spiders had been renamed the Indians, and Cy Young was not exactly young anymore, but he was happy to be back in Cleveland, close to home. Although the Indians were a sixth-place team, Young worked his regular turn and

ck in a Cleveland uniform 1909, the 42-year-old ung led the team in tories with 19.

Young was one of the best control pitchers of all time. From 1893 to 1906, he led the league 11 times in fewest walks per nine innings. He finished second the other two years.

managed to win 19 games while losing 15. Old Cy Young was getting heavier around the middle, and it was harder for him to cover his position, fielding bunts and slow rollers. But his arm was still strong. Only three pitchers in the American League bettered Young's 1908 record, and only three worked more innings.

By 1910, his arm seemed to be going and he had to rely more on his smarts to get the batters out. For only the third time in 21 years, he lost more games than he won: 7-10. He pitched only 163 innings, down from 295 just a year earlier.

The highlight of the season for Young came on July 18, when he won his 500th game. He had to work 11 innings to earn the victory. After giving up just one hit in eight innings, he weakened in the 9th and Washington tied the score, 2–2. But then the Indians scored 3 runs in the 11th for the win.

When Cy Young returned to the farm that fall, it looked as if his days of long bumpy train rides and hours passed in hotel lobbies were over. But the Indians sent him a contract for 1911 in the hope that he could still win a few games for them—and draw a lot of fans. In midseason, with Young's record at 3-4, they decided to give his place to a younger pitcher. Released in August, Young was disappointed. Yet he was happy to be returning to the farm.

His journey home was cut short, however, by an offer to return to Boston, this time as one of the National League Braves. Probably no other offer could have tempted him, but he had been happy in Boston and eagerly returned there. The Braves figured that even an old Cy Young was good enough to bring people into the park. And they were correct. Cy was still the fans' favorite.

COMPLIMENTARY DINNER

GIVEN BY

CY YOUNG

TO THE MEMBERS OF THE

BOSTON AMERICAN BASE BALL CLUB

STUDENTS' SPA
PUTNAM HOUSE
BOSTON, MASS
SEPT. 15, 1908

Menu

♣

BLUE POINTS, LAKE STYLE

GREEN OLIVES   WOOD'S CELERY   BRADY RADISHES

CONSOMMÉ À LA SULLIVAN

BOILED FRESH SALMON, CRIGER SAUCE
THONEY CUCUMBERS   NILES TOMATOES   KELLEY POTATOES

FRESH PUTNAM FARM CHICKEN, CY YOUNG STYLE
STAHL POTATOES   GESSLER JELLY

PLANKED SIRLOIN STEAK, AU DONAHUE DRESSING
ARELLANES FRITTERS   WAGNER GLACE
HIGGINS POTATOES   JERRY PEAS   LORD'S STRING BEANS

SPRING SALAD À LA BURCHELL

PLUM PUDDING, STEELE SAUCE

CICOTTE SUNDAE   CRAVATH CAKES
HOEY RAISINS   SPEAKER'S SALTED NUTS   CARRIGAN GRAPES

McMAHON'S CHEESE   McCONNELL'S CRACKERS
AMERICAN LEAGUE STYLE

MORGAN COFFEE   CIGARS

In his first outing back in Boston, Young was hit hard. Yet when manager Fred Tenney took him out, the crowd loudly booed the move.

Young went on to win just four games for the Braves while losing five. Still, he showed flashes of greatness even in defeat. On September 7, the Braves met the Phillies and Young wound up in a pitchers' duel against future Hall of Famer Grover Cleveland Alexander. For nine innings, both pitchers retired the batters without a run. The 44-year-old veteran kept pace with the 24-year-old rookie through the 10th and 11th, but the Phillies scratched out a run in the 12th to win 1–0.

Two weeks later, the powerful Pirates reached Young for 9 hits, but he bore down and shut them out, 1–0. It was the first time he had pitched in Pittsburgh since the 1903 World

As a way of thanking the Boston players for giving him his "day," Young hosted a dinner at the Putnam Hotel in September 1908. Each of the dishes on the menu is named after a teammate.

Series. And it was his last win, number 511. He had won more games than most pitchers would ever hurl. It is a record that still stands today.

On October 6, Young held Brooklyn in check for six innings but gave up seven runs and eight hits in the 7th. Unable to get that elusive last out, he finally tossed the ball to a relief pitcher young enough to be his son and strolled to the clubhouse for the last time. It was loss number 315 for him. He had pitched so many games (906) over 22 years that he had also *lost* more than anybody else.

The Braves invited Young to spring training in 1912, but his arm felt as heavy as a pump handle and he was slow moving on the field. He had always hated the grind of spring training, calling it "the most irksome duty that I encounter, and only a little short of the most exquisite

In the early 1940s, Cy relaxed while his young friend Jane Benedum sat behind the wheel of his car. The trophies on display are now in the Baseball Hall of Fame.

agony." Now, at the age of 45, it was all agony.

"The boys are taking unfair advantage of an old man," Young said ruefully. "They know this big stomach of mine makes it difficult for me to field bunts, so instead of swinging at my stuff, they are laying the ball down. When the third baseman has to start doing my work, it's time for me to quit."

Back on the farm, Young talked about getting into better shape and returning to the mound, but he never did. He had pitched 7,356 innings and 750 complete games (two more records yet to be broken), and that was enough for any man.

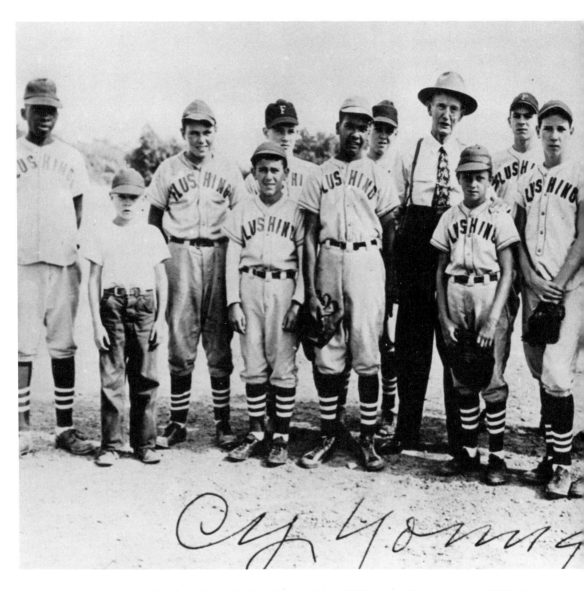

Cy Young, in a photograph taken shortly before his death in 1955, was a big supporter of Little League baseball. The official program for the 1956 Little League World Series included a tribute to Cy Young. It read, in part:

One month after he delivered a strike pitch to open the 1955 World Series, Denton T. Young, oldest of all the Little Leaguers, was laid to rest in the quiet peace of an Ohio hillside.

This week, there is an empty chair in the sun, back of third base, and for all of us there will be a priceless memory of baseball's greatest pitcher who once occupied it.

8

THE CY YOUNG
AWARD

Cy Young received several offers to coach and manage, but they did not interest him. He was content to remain a part of the small-town life that revolved around the seasons: farm work, hunting, local ballgames, and Saturday night socializing at the Elks Club.

After his wife died in 1933, Young was a lonely man. He invited close family friends, Mr. and Mrs. John Benedum and their young daughter, Jane, to come live with him. But without his wife the homestead he had built did not mean much to him anymore. He became restless.

When a chance came along to lead a team of oldtimers on a tour, Young jumped at it. He sold the farm and auctioned off most of his personal belongings. The Benedums bought a nearby farm of their own. But the tour was not successful and was soon abandoned. Young returned to Tuscarawas County, but he no longer had any land on which to take root. He lived for a while in a hotel room. When the Benedums suggested he make his home with them, he readily accepted. He felt good chopping wood, husking corn, and doing all the old familiar chores. The brightest star in his life became the Benedums' little girl, Jane. He rocked her to sleep when she was a baby and guided her on real piggyback rides on the pigs in the yard. Cy Young and Jane Benedum were great pals as the little girl grew up, and they remained close for the rest of the pitcher's life.

Cy Young was elected to the Hall of Fame in 1937. When its museum opened two years later, he joined the other stars of his day who gathered for the first formal induction ceremony at Cooperstown, New York.

In 1938, Young received a letter from Frederick Putnam, the man who had opened a hotel in Boston at Young's suggestion 38 years earlier. Putnam had enlarged the hotel and now wanted his old friend to come work for him as a "greeter." It would be Young's job to bring people into the hotel after the ballgames. Young was eager for work and he still liked Boston, so he accepted Putnam's offer. But the late nights were contrary to his lifelong habits, and he missed his friend Jane. Less that a year later, he was back in Peoli.

Young kept in touch with the world of baseball and regularly appeared at induction ceremonies for new entrants into the Hall of Fame at Cooperstown. He also attended games in Cleveland and was always good for an interview and an opinion about the game. But most of his time was spent at home, felling trees and splitting rails for fences, cutting corn, husking, haypitching, and harvesting. In his late seventies, he could still outsaw many younger men on one end of a cross-cut saw.

On March 29, 1947, Young's neighbors tossed a party for his 80th birthday. More than 800 people showed up for a roast beef dinner, which

Baseball Commissioner Ford Frick, troubled by the lack of pitchers winning the Most Valuable Player Award, helped initiate the Cy Young Award in 1956 to recognize the outstanding pitcher each year. Ironically, the first winner was the Dodgers' Don Newcombe, who also won the N.L.'s MVP trophy.

was provided by two steers raised by Young. A huge birthday cake, 80 inches in diameter and 5 feet high, blazed with 80 candles. The crowd was so large the people had to be fed in five different places. Afterward, everyone reassembled for the rest of the festivities. The governor gave a speech, and Cleveland Indians owner Bill Veeck signed Cy to an honorary contract.

Two of Young's teammates from the 1890 Canton team were there to pay him tribute, along with former Yankee pitchers Waite Hoyt and Sam Jones. "I was a fair big-league pitcher if I do say it myself," said Hoyt. "And I won only 238 games. Sam Jones won 237 in 22 years. We know, Sam and I, probably better than any person present, what it means to have won 511 games."

But Cy Young was still not quite finished with the game. When Little League baseball began

Cy Young's 1910 Old Mill tobacco card.

around 1949, he quickly became interested in helping to promote the idea. One of the first things he said to the program's organizers was, "Get the kids the equipment, uniforms and bats and balls, but make them earn it. I never saw a loafing ballplayer in my time who was ever any good. And that goes back to the first professional game I ever played. Even if the kids you sponsor are only 10 years old, get a program for them that will make them hustle every minute."

The 82-year-old Hall of Famer traveled to many states for meetings, banquets, and special games. Some people were concerned that he was too old to hold the interest of boys and their fathers as a speaker, but Young knew how to capture an audience. At one dinner, he was asked to demonstrate how he held a ball when he pitched. He picked up a roll, showed how he palmed it for different pitches, then wound up and flung it clear across the room. Wherever he went after that, somebody would always ask him to show how he threw the ball: It became the most popular part of the program.

For young pitchers he had this advice: "Don't loaf during the winter. You don't have to exercise your arm, that will take care of itself. But run and work hard to keep your body tough the year round. A good solid constitution will do more for your athletic career than all the skill you may possess.... A beginner should work for a long time on straight balls alone. This does not seem very exciting, but it contains a big secret that many overlook. The beginner should keep throwing this straight ball until he can absolutely put the ball where the catcher wants it. Next, cultivate a slow ball, and get control of that; it makes no difference how long it takes, get control of it before you go on with something else."

In 1955, at the age of 88, Young was asked to throw out the first ball at the Little League World Series. When he got to the mound he threw aside his cane, wound up, and fired a perfect strike. The cheers of the crowd were as sweet to his ears as any he had heard in the big leagues.

One month later, on November 4, 1955, at home in Peoli, Cy Young fell asleep in an easy chair and did not wake up.

The man who was as sturdy as the oak trees he walked beneath, was buried beside his wife on a hilltop overlooking the farmland he loved. He was not a wealthy man, and he left very little money. But he left something of far greater value.

For many years, there had been a controversy about the Most Valuable Player Awards bestowed by baseball writers on the player in each league who had made the greatest contribution to his team's success. Occasionally, a pitcher would win it, but most writers thought that a player who did not play every day could not be as valuable as a regular, no matter how outstanding his performance.

This did not seem fair to baseball's commissioner Ford Frick, and in 1956 he inaugurated an annual award just for pitchers. Because Young had been baseball's biggest winner, the only pitcher to win 200 or more games in both major leagues, it was only fitting that the trophy be called the Cy Young Award. Until 1965, only one pitcher a year was honored; then the present practice began of naming a winner in each league. To this day, it remains the highest honor a pitcher can earn. And to this day, Cy Young remains baseball's winningest pitcher.

CHRONOLOGY

Mar. 29, 1867	Cy Young is born on a farm near Gilmore, Ohio
Apr. 30, 1890	Pitches first professional game for Canton, (in the Tri-State League), a 4–2 win against Wheeling
Aug. 6, 1890	Pitches first major league game, for Cleveland, beating Chicago, 8–1
Nov. 8, 1892	Marries Robba Miller
Sept. 18, 1897	Pitches first no-hitter, 6-0, against Cincinnati
Apr. 25, 1901	Pitches first opener for Boston Americans
Oct. 1, 1903	Throws first pitch in modern World Series but loses the game to Pittsburgh
May 5, 1904	Pitches perfect game, 3-0, against Athletics
May 11, 1904	Sets record of $23^2/_3$ consecutive hitless innings
July 4, 1905	Loses 20-inning game, 4-2, to Rube Waddell and the Athletics
June 30, 1908	Pitches third no-hitter, 8-0, against New York
Aug. 13, 1908	Cy Young Day is celebrated in Boston
July 18, 1910	Wins 500th game, 5-2, against Washington
Sept. 22, 1911	Wins 511th and last game, 1-0, against Pittsburgh
1937	Elected to Hall of Fame
Nov. 4, 1955	Dies at home in Peoli, Ohio

DENTON T. (CY) YOUNG
CLEVELAND (N) 1890-98
ST. LOUIS (N) 1899-1900
BOSTON (A) 1901-08
CLEVELAND (A) 1909-11
BOSTON (N) 1911
ONLY PITCHER IN FIRST HUNDRED
YEARS OF BASEBALL TO WIN 500 GAMES.
AMONG HIS 511 VICTORIES WERE 3
NO-HIT SHUTOUTS. PITCHED PERFECT
GAME MAY 5, 1904, NO OPPOSING
BATSMAN REACHING FIRST BASE.

MAJOR LEAGUE STATISTICS

CLEVELAND INDIANS, ST. LOUIS CARDINALS, BOSTON RED SOX, BOSTON BRAVES

YEAR	TEAM	W	L	PCT	ERA	G	GS	CG	IP	H	BB	SO	ShO
1890	Cle N	9	6	.600	3.47	17	16	16	147.2	145	30	39	0
1891		27	22	.551	2.85	55	46	43	423.2	431	140	147	0
1892		36	12	.750	1.93	53	49	48	453	363	118	168	9
1893		34	16	.680	3.36	53	46	42	422.2	442	103	102	1
1894		26	21	.553	3.94	52	47	44	408.2	488	106	101	2
1895		35	10	.778	3.24	47	40	36	369.2	363	75	121	4
1896		28	15	.651	3.24	51	46	42	414.1	477	62	140	5
1897		21	19	.525	3.79	46	38	35	335	391	49	88	2
1898		25	13	.658	2.53	46	41	40	377.2	387	41	101	1
1899	Stl N	26	16	.619	2.58	44	42	40	369.1	368	44	111	4
1900		19	19	.500	3.00	41	35	32	321.1	337	36	115	4
1901	Bos A	33	10	.767	1.62	43	41	38	371.1	324	37	158	5
1902		32	11	.744	2.15	45	43	41	384.2	350	53	160	3
1903		28	9	.757	2.08	40	35	34	341.2	294	37	176	7
1904		26	16	.619	1.97	43	41	40	380	327	29	200	10
1905		18	19	.486	1.82	38	33	32	320.2	248	30	210	4
1906		13	21	.382	3.19	39	34	28	287.2	288	25	140	0
1907		21	15	.583	1.99	43	37	33	343.1	286	51	147	6
1908		21	11	.656	1.26	36	33	30	299	230	37	150	3
1909	Cle A	19	15	.559	2.26	35	34	30	295	267	59	109	3
1910		7	10	.412	2.53	21	20	14	163.1	149	27	58	1
1911	2 teams		Cle A (7G)		Bos N (11G)								
	total	7	9	.438	3.78	18	18	12	126.1	137	28	55	2
Totals		511	315	.619	2.63	906	815	750	7356	7092	1217	2796	76
World Series													
1903	Bos A	2	1	.667	1.59	4	3	3	34	31	4	17	0

FURTHER READING

Allen, Lee & Meany, Tom. *Kings of the Diamond.* New York: G. P. Putnam, 1965.

Broeg, Bob. *Super Stars of Baseball.* St. Louis: The Sporting News, 1971.

Charlton, James. *The Baseball Chronology.* New York: Macmillan, 1991.

Meany, Tom. *Baseball's Greatest Pitchers.* New York: A. S. Barnes, 1953.

Romig, Ralph. *Cy Young: Baseball's Legendary Giant.* Philadelphia: Dorrance, 1964.

Shapiro, Milton J. *Baseball's Greatest Pitchers.* New York: Julian Messner, 1969.

Smith, Ira L. *Baseball's Famous Pitchers.* New York: A. S. Barnes, 1954.

Walsh, Christy. *Baseball's Greatest Lineup.* New York: A. S. Barnes, 1952.

Wind, Herbert W. *The Realm of Sport.* New York: Simon & Schuster, 1966.

INDEX

PICTURE CREDIT

National Baseball Library, Cooperstown, NY: pp. 2, 8, 14, 16, 19, 22, 24, 26, 40, 44, 46, 48, 50, 52, 55, 58, 60; Northeastern University, World Series Room: pp. 11, 29, 30, 32, 35, 36, 38, 43, 49; From the collection of James Charlton: p. 56

NORMAN L. MACHT was a minor league general manager with the Milwaukee Braves and Baltimore Orioles organizations and has been a stockbroker and college professor. His work has appeared in *The BallPlayers*, *The Sporting News*, *Baseball Digest* and *Sports Heritage*, and he is the co-author with Dick Bartell of *Rowdy Richard*. Norman Macht lives in Newark, Delaware.

JIM MURRAY, veteran sports columnist of the *Los Angeles Times*, is one of America's most acclaimed writers. He has been named "America's Best Sportswriter" by the National Association of Sportscasters and Sportswriters 14 times, was awarded the Red Smith Award, and was twice winner of the National Headliner Award. In addition, he was awarded the J. G. Taylor Spink Award in 1987 for "meritorious contributions to baseball writing." With this award came his 1988 induction into the National Baseball Hall of Fame in Cooperstown, New York. In 1990, Jim Murray was awarded the Pulitzer Prize for Commentary.

EARL WEAVER is the winningest manager in Baltimore Orioles history by a wide margin. He compiled 1,480 victories in his 17 years at the helm. After managing eight different minor league teams, he was given the chance to lead the Orioles in 1968. Under his leadership the Orioles finished lower than second place in the American League East only four times in 17 years. One of only 12 managers in big league history to have managed in four or more World Series, Earl was named Manager of the Year in 1979. The popular Weaver had his number 4 retired in 1982, joining Brooks Robinson, Frank Robinson, and Jim Palmer, whose numbers were retired previously. Earl Weaver continues his association with the professional baseball scene by writing, broadcasting, and coaching.